Original title:
Between Floorboards and Roofbeams

Copyright © 2025 Creative Arts Management OÜ
All rights reserved.

Author: Julian Carmichael
ISBN HARDBACK: 978-1-80587-068-5
ISBN PAPERBACK: 978-1-80587-538-3

Residue of Lives Lived Below

Lost socks dance in the dark,
Old bills whisper sweet remarks.
A sandwich, crusty with time,
Holds secrets aged like fine wine.

An odd shoe sits on the stair,
With no partner, it just stares.
What did it witness, who knows?
Perhaps a cat, or even prose!

Timelessness in the Crannies

Dust bunnies hold a grand parade,
While spiders knit with thread they've made.
Each corner packed with laughter's trace,
Embraced by shadow's soft embrace.

A rogue marble rolls away,
It's on a quest, come what may.
In every crack, a grin awaits,
As time tiptoes, and fate creates.

A Whisper Across the Plaster

Voices echo through the walls,
As echoes tumble, laughter calls.
A picture frame slips from its hoop,
Daring gravity with a swoop.

Chipped paint tells a silly tale,
Of old cats who never fail.
They plot to pounce at night's delight,
While mice convene in sheer fright!

Untold Stories of Joists and Beams

Joists hum with ballads old,
While beams boast of jumps bold.
They've cradled dreams, held laughter tight,
Underneath the starlit night.

A whimsical dance by the pipe,
In a world where few dare type.
If you listen close, you'll hear
The symphony of laughter near.

The Beneath and the Above

In the attic, dust bunnies dance,
While cobwebs spin their silk romance.
A raccoon hosts a wild, late-night ball,
With snacks of forgotten food — oh, what a haul!

Under the floor, secrets burrow,
Lost socks and crumbs, steadfast as a furrow.
A mouse runs a bakery, perhaps just for fun,
Bakery smells waft when day is done.

Dreams Weave Through the Planks

A creaky board sings a lullaby,
While old nails dream of the sky.
The beams above wear a dust throne,
With spirits of laughter — never alone.

In the corners, shadows play peek-a-boo,
Whispering jokes that only they knew.
The chimney sways, wearing a hat of soot,
Such a regal chimney, who'd ever think it could?

The Hidden Symphony of Shelter

A roof hums softly with each raindrop's glee,
Pattering rhythms, a musical spree.
In the walls, squirrels compose their own score,
Chasing echoes that bounce off the floor.

Under the stairs, a concert unfolds,
As forgotten treasures spin tales of old.
The rattling pipes join in a quirky tune,
While sunlight dances like a jovial moon.

In the Gaps Where Stories Breathe

A mouthy gap squeaks and squeals,
As floorboards share their spinning reels.
Whispers of mischief crawl through the seams,
Tickling the edges of half-formed dreams.

Above, the rafters hold their breath tight,
Eavesdropping on birds and their morning flight.
Chuckles erupt from the rafters so high,
As they fall with the dust, in a cloud-like sigh.

Whispers of Hidden Spaces

In nooks where dust bunnies play,
A sock puppet sings far away.
Mice throw parties, cheese in tow,
With little hats, they steal the show.

Under the stairs, a dragon snores,
While grandma's yarn becomes a war.
Kid's old toys dance in the gloom,
Chasing shadows that fill the room.

Shadows in the Attic

Up in the attic, a treasure trove,
Of mismatched hats and grandma's stove.
A ghost in a wig gives a wink,
While old toys plot, or so we think.

A mannequin waves with a friendly smile,
Dancing with cobwebs all the while.
Old records spin tales of cheer,
As the dust bunnies party, oh dear!

Unseen Tales of the Home

Walls whisper secrets of things long gone,
Where dust settles softly at the dawn.
The tea kettle cheers with a joyful steam,
As spoons make music—a lively dream.

Behind the fridge, a sock brigade,
Planning their escape, a grand parade.
A rogue goldfish has taken flight,
In a cereal bowl, it swims with delight.

Echoes of Forgotten Corners

In the corner, an old broom sighs,
Dreaming of flights and midnight skies.
The cat's in league with the cupboard mice,
Plotting together, oh how nice!

A chair that creaks tells of ancient tales,
Of ghosts and laughter, and forgotten trails.
The clock ticks softly, keeping time,
With secrets wrapped in laughter and rhyme.

Where Shadows Gather

In corners where the dust bunnies play,
Socks come to life in a grand cabaret.
With dust motes dancing a cheeky ballet,
And the cat's judging with a stern, 'No way!'

A creak in the floor makes a ghostly sound,
But it's just the squeaky toy that's been found.
It wiggles and giggles, not making a bound,
As laughter erupts from the cluttered ground.

Layers of Light and Dark

Under the stairs, the treasures abound,
With old toys and shoes that we thought we'd drowned.
A pirate hat here and an old cape is found,
Where mismatched socks wish they were renowned.

The light flickers on with a mischievous glow,
As shadows form figures in a playful show.
A dance party erupts, oh what a tableau,
With crumbs from the cookies that vanished below.

The Echo of Footfalls

Each step on the stairs is a riddle to crack,
As slippers and sneakers wage their own attack.
The echoes collide with a flip and a quack,
A parade of old memories wearing a sack.

Tapping and slapping on wooden expanse,
It's a rhythm of childhood that gives us a chance.
To spin, twirl, and leap in a whimsical dance,
While the cat looks on like, 'What's this romance?'

Whispers in the Wainscot

In the wainscot's depth, secrets murmur low,
Of muffins that vanished and hats in a row.
The mice hold a meeting, their voice soft like snow,
Planning a feast with crumbs from the dough.

With giggles and whispers, the walls tell a tale,
Of pranks played by children, their laughter a gale.
The dust laughs along, while the floorboards turn pale,
As the room takes a breath, in a soft, cozy veil.

Chasing Shadows in Quiet Date

In the attic where dust bunnies roam,
Came a draft that seemed to call me home.
I tiptoed past boxes stacked on high,
With whispers of secrets, I couldn't deny.

Laughter erupted from a creaky chair,
As it squeaked like a cat, brightened the air.
Caught in a dance with shadows so bold,
A living room circus, or so I'm told.

The clock chimed a tune that was terribly wrong,
It sang like a bird that had lost its song.
Mice tapped their feet in a rhythmic display,
And I joined their jig in a curious sway.

As the sun set, and the whispers grew deep,
I chuckled at floorboards that never could sleep.
For in that cozy chaos, I found my spree,
In this wacky dance of unending glee.

The Interstice of Silence

In corners where echoes left secrets unspun,
A sock found a friend in a wayward bun.
They argued all night about who'd been lost,
The sock claimed it mattered, the bun just glossed.

The silence was thick, like a fog in a dream,
With crickets composing an awkward theme.
They painted the walls with their serenade,
While the lamp sighed in shadows, in deep masquerade.

The chair forged a rumor it used to be spry,
While the pictures hung still, like they just can't lie.
And here in this living, between things that stick,
I heard the floor whisper a cheeky little trick.

Out from the pantry, a pickle tried to dance,
Stumbling and joyful, it seized its chance.
In this curious space of chuckles and sighs,
Silence held court, with a twinkle in its eyes.

An Archive of Light and Space

Beneath the glow of a flickering bulb,
Old memories shuffled, like they were ambled.
Dust motes in sunlight, a waltz in the air,
While cobwebs giggled, as if they could stare.

The couch recited tales of oh so long past,
When biscuits were thrown and laughter amassed.
The carpet's soft voice shared a story of spills,
Of a soda explosion that echoed in thrills.

A lamp with a shade, sporting an ancient stain,
Blinked at the curtains, a silent campaign.
The cat on the windowsill flicked her tail,
As moths danced around, spinning tales in detail.

In this archive of light, a mishmash of time,
Where beams hold the stories of guffaws and grime,
I found in the corners, a playful embrace,
Laughter persists in this haunted space.

Memories Caught in the Rafters

In the attic, a squirrel's stash,
Old toys dancing, a quirky clash.
Grandma's quilt, a patchwork tale,
Whispers of giggles, adventures prevail.

A calendar with cats in hats,
Beneath it, piles of dusty mats.
Laughter echoes from the past,
Each corner holds a memory cast.

A broomstick ride, a grand parade,
Secret treasures, where fears once laid.
Old boots waiting for a stroll,
Each faded step, a cherished role.

Who knew the rafters had a flair,
For secrets shared beyond compare?
Looming shadows dance and play,
As time rolls on and dreams decay.

Dust Motions in the Sunlight

Sunbeams stretch through window panes,
    Catch the dust like silly trains.
  Floating figures, a lovely sight,
    Twinkle toes in golden light.

A sneeze erupts, the dance is paused,
The dust bunnies blink, feeling awed.
Unearthing jokes from hidden nooks,
    With every beam, laughter cooks.

They swirl and spin, a comical spree,
    Imitating clouds, wild and free.
    In every speck, a chuckle grows,
  As time drifts by in soft repose.

  A motley crew of lazy dreams,
Chasing each other, or so it seems.
Who knew the dust could wear a crown?
  With every wave, it won't back down.

The Stories We Build

Under stairs where secrets hide,
A fort of pillows, our hearts abide.
Bonkers tales, we weave them high,
Pirates, fairies, oh my, oh my!

Lego towers scrape the sky,
Imagination soars, oh why?
Each toppled block brings silly glee,
Creating worlds, just you and me.

Mom's old chair, a throne one day,
Magic spins in absurd ballet.
Tea parties with imaginary friends,
Where laughter, like confetti, descends.

We craft our dreams with dirt and cheer,
Sharing snickers, conquering fear.
In every crack, a bold new scheme,
Life's a play, we're on the beam!

Beneath the Surface of Shelter

Underneath where shadows dwell,
A curious mouse prepares to tell.
About lost crumbs and midnight feasts,
In the ballet of odd little beasts.

A sock has gone, but never alone,
The cat claims it as a throne.
Tales of mischief in each stitch,
A fabric story, rich and rich.

Boxes stacked like towers tall,
What treasures wait, who can recall?
Past homespun dreams and cozy nights,
Crafting laughter with silly sights.

What secrets brew where dust bunnies trot?
A circus of ghosts, oh, what a plot!
So raise a cup to the unseen cheer,
For in our hearts, they all draw near.

Ghosts of Sudden Raindrops

Drops tap dance on the windowsill,
Ghosts pulling pranks with joyful thrill.
Umbrellas grow legs, jump and sway,
While puddles giggle, come out to play.

Drenched squirrels slide down the tree,
   Chasing shadows, wild and free.
They trade their acorns for soggy bread,
And laugh at the chaos, unafraid to tread.

Secrets Held in the Beams

Up in the attic, whispers abound,
Old hats and boxes, treasures unbound.
A time-traveling cat with a yarn of tales,
Spins stories of pirates in leaky gales.

Dust bunnies giggle, conspiracy plotted,
As creaky wood chuckles, never delotted.
What lies up there, who can be sure?
Fluffy secrets from days of yore.

The Craft of Ancestral Silence

Grandma's knitting needles click in the dark,
Reviving old anecdotes, lighting a spark.
Once upon a time, with a wink and a nudge,
She cast magic, which made the curtains fudge.

From behind the couch, a shadow does peek,
A great-great-grandpa with hiccups to leak.
Weird recipes whispered, with giggles on cue,
Tales of a stew made with my great-aunt's shoe.

Footfalls in the Quiet Loft

Step by step, the floorboards creak,
In the quiet loft, the ghosts like to sneak.
With mismatched socks and hats askew,
They plot pranks on the ones they knew.

The old rocking chair starts to sway,
As if to say, 'Come join the play!'
But when you peek to catch a glance,
It's just a cat caught in a dance.

Veils of Time in Tight Places

Dust bunnies dance in the corner,
They've been partying since last summer.
Old shoes tell tales of lost events,
While socks plot their great escape attempts.

A spider spins webs with such flair,
Hosting brunch for flies with no care.
The cat gives a sigh, a lazy sprawl,
While echoes of giggles bounce off the wall.

Beneath the old bed, secrets await,
Whispers of mischief that time can't abate.
A cereal box, knocked and forlorn,
Once a fortress for knights, now just torn.

In the attic, a treasure trove lies,
With forgotten dolls and outlandish ties.
Each item a jester, a clue in disguise,
Offering laughter as the past slowly flies.

The Breath of Hidden Nooks

Slippers wiggle in corners they hide,
Murmurs of mischief, where secrets reside.
A shoehorn stands like a knight in its prime,
Protecting old tales that dance out of time.

The closet door creaks with stories untold,
Of embarrassing outfits, and bags made of gold.
Each sweater holds wisdom, each belt, a fit,
The adventures of wearers, all lined up to sit.

In shadows, the dust becomes fables anew,
Of long-lost romances and wild rendezvous.
The mirrors reflect on intentions quite sly,
If only they'd gossip, oh, what a reply!

How socks may be sinners, or heroes in wait,
Each with a story on their pre-loved plate.
They all share their laughter, their glee and delight,
In the breath of the nooks, where all seems just right.

Imprints of Lives Lived

Footprints linger on dusty old floors,
Each step a giggle, each creak a roar.
Beneath the old carpet, a maze they construct,
With daring adventures and snacks they abduct.

In the kitchen, crumbs form a map on the counter,
Leading to tales of the great cookie bounty.
A spatula sings of breakfast delights,
While forks share secrets of late-night bites.

The back door swings wide, a portal of cheer,
As laughter escapes and memories appear.
Each window a frame for the past's gentle play,
Where imprints of lives lived dance in ballet.

A mantle adorned with odd trinkets of lore,
Tells of mischief and antics galore.
Dust motes perform in the soft morning light,
As history's laughter echoes through the night.

Crumbs of History in the Quiet

Creaky stairs whisper of stories so sweet,
From children's footsteps to pet paws that greet.
Each step is a melody, each squeak a chime,
A timeline of chaos, ticking in rhyme.

Under the table lie treasures once lost,
Forgotten confidences, at little cost.
Old napkins hold secrets from dinners long gone,
While forks and spoons banter till the break of dawn.

Dust gathers gently, the ghosts do their dance,
In corners where puddles of laughter still prance.
A teacup's still smiling, with tales in its rim,
Of clinks and of clatters, now faded and dim.

The clock on the wall quietly snickers away,
Counting the giggles of yesterday's play.
In this hush of the house, life's crumbs gather round,
As echoes of joy in the silence abound.

Lullabies in the Shadows

In hidden nooks, the critters hum,
A chorus faint, where shadows drum.
Dust bunnies dance, a jig so bright,
While ceiling fans spin tales at night.

A mouse with dreams of cheese delight,
Whispers secrets to the moonlight.
The creaky floor applauds the show,
In this grand theatre down below.

The cobwebs sway, a soft ballet,
As spiders weave their yarns each day.
Light bulbs flicker like giggles shared,
As laughter lingers, fully bared.

So when you drift to sleep away,
Remember this, the critters play.
For in the dark, joy's not so far,
Just listen close, they're never bizarre.

The Forgotten Cornices Call

Up high they sit, the cornices sigh,
With tales of old that wink and pry.
They gossip soft as dust drifts down,
In whispers sweet on sleepy towns.

When you think they're just decor,
Listen close – they've so much more!
A laugh, a cheer, a playful tease,
From ancient wood, they never freeze.

They chuckle at the spills and stains,
Of every life that shares their planes.
A toast to all the years gone by,
With memories held in every sigh.

So gaze aloft, give pause to hear,
The whispers that drift, ever near.
For every crack has stories grand,
In architecture's playful hand.

The Veil of Soft Dust

In corners thick, the dust does play,
With tiny worlds where fairies lay.
It blankets all in gentle fray,
And tickles noses, come what may.

When beams of light start to cascade,
The dust transforms, an art parade.
Sprites adorned in glittering gown,
They rule the stage, they wear the crown.

A sneezing fit, the puppets fall,
The dust bunnies laugh, they had a ball!
For every tickle brings new cheer,
In the soft veil of what's unclear.

So next you see a dust mote swirl,
Just know it's not a simple whirl.
It's magic spun from laughter's grace,
In every nook, a smiling face.

Fragments of Love in the Frames

The photos hang with smiles bright,
Caught in time, a pure delight.
Yet whispered tales of love gone strange,
Beneath the glass, lives rearrange.

The outfits change, but hearts still beat,
In frames adorned, life's merry feat.
Grandma's wiggle, grandpa's grin,
Those awkward hugs, where do we begin?

Each frame a story, some absurd,
With love expressed in actions heard.
A cat that stole the limelight there,
With playful pounces, quite the affair.

So when you peek at snapshots past,
Remember love's a merry cast.
In fleeting moments held so tight,
Life's portrait shines with pure delight.

Breaths of History Stored Away

Dust bunnies dance, oh what a sight,
Each corner holds secrets that tickle the night.
An old shoe whispers with a creak and a sigh,
While the kitchen mouse chuckles, as neighbors pass by.

The attic's a circus of long-forgotten hats,
Where dreams of old clowns tumble with rats.
A sock puppet's laughter built with old yarn,
Invites every ghost to a show on the lawn.

Under the rug lies a treasure of crumbs,
Moldy delights, remnants of sandwiches from chums.
Laughter echoes as memories unfold,
In the corners of rooms where stories are told.

With each creak of the floor, a tale takes flight,
Of rogue kittens bounding in the soft moonlight.
The house giggles softly, a silly old chap,
Cradling each jest in a cozy, warm lap.

The Unseen Lives of Walls

Walls whisper in hues of faded delight,
Collecting the laughter long into the night.
Where spackle and paint play a quirky game,
As family dinners usher in wild acclaim.

Oh, the stories they hold with a knowing grin,
Like a cat's lazy stretch or a toddler's spin.
Where pictures lean sideways, a sight full of glee,
Reminiscing of moments, like 'Who let that bee?'

Behind every shimmer, a tale softly waits,
Of childhood adventures and polka dot plates.
The jiggles and wiggles of shady old frames,
Giggle and tease, but forget all the names.

In echoes of parties, a faint song remains,
While the varnished wood chuckles with gentle refrains.
A slice of old pizza and crumbs on the ledge,
Mark the fine history held at the edge.

Stories Trapped in Timber

Oh, timber, you've seen some marvelous things,
From dances with dust to the laughter of kings.
While termites take notes on the jokes that you weave,
Rustling old leaves, they plot and conceive.

A bird once nested, with dreams bold and bright,
Where branches would sway, a whimsical sight.
And the squirrels would chatter, oh what a sound,
As woodpeckers knocked out the beat all around.

In your veins, there lies a wild family tree,
Of wooden legacies, full of jubilee.
Every scratch and every groove tells a tale,
Of mischief and magic, of treasure and trail.

Time's funny trickster, it tickles your bark,
With laughter that echoes from dawn until dark.
Oh, the stories that whisper in knots and in grain,
Invite every heart to enjoy the refrain.

Murmurs from the Underlayment

Down below where the shadows creep,
The underlayment chuckles, secrets to keep.
Old nails gossip, with squeaks they unite,
Conspiracies spinning, all through the night.

A ruckus of whispers from padding and scruff,
Tell tales of spilled drinks and enough is enough!
Cramped spaces where dust bunnies dare to invade,
Plotting their schemes in cloaks that they made.

Wires hum softly, in electronic duet,
While mischievous roaches launch dance floors on yet.
Each pluck and each tickle, a fun little dance,
Bringing forth laughter, if given a chance.

Beneath all the weight of the world up above,
Lives a community thriving on silliness, love.
So listen closely, as the floors start to play,
For joy can be found in the strange and array.

The Space Where Light Meets Dark

A sock that vanished from the wash,
Now mingles with dust and a small old posh.
It giggles in shadows where no one can see,
In corners of laughter, where whispers run free.

A mouse with a hat plays chess with a cat,
Both lost in their moves, peach pie on the mat.
The ceiling fan spins tales from days of yore,
As light and dark tango, they dance on the floor.

The curtain sings softly, so wrinkled and loose,
It tells of each party and wine-drunk sprouse.
A light bulb flickers, an old friend nearby,
With secrets in whispers that light on the sly.

So let's raise a toast to shadows that play,
To socks and to mice that won't fade away.
In the warm space where chuckles and whispers collide,
Is the room of forgotten, where dreams still reside.

Nostalgia in the Moulding

The grandpa clock snores in a corner so neat,
While spiders weave blankets in threads bittersweet.
Each tick is a laugh from the past that once rolled,
As memories linger, both comical and bold.

The wallpaper peels like a smile that's worn,
It carries old stories, a trifle forlorn.
A yo-yo lost long in the wake of a race,
Hangs out with the marbles in a jubilant place.

An old shoelace stretched by a cat's silly pounce,
Dances with dust motes that spin and then bounce.
Beneath the old oak beams, where shadows delight,
Nostalgia throws parties, well into the night.

From creaks in the floor to the crack in the wall,
The echoes of laughter come calling for all.
So raise up a cheer for the past's funny charm,
For moments of whimsy, let's keep them warm.

Reveries Lost in the Rafters

In the attic, the whispers of old fluffy hats,
Share tales of romance with runaway cats.
A trunk full of dreams waits in still dusty haze,
As memories giggle in sunlight's soft rays.

The ghosts of old mittens play catch with the moon,
While echoes of laughter hum an old tune.
A wooden shoe tap dances, one shoe on its own,
While shadows of hats hold a raucous bone throne.

Old toy trains rumble on thoughts that can't die,
As visions of laughter swirl up to the sky.
The rafters hold secrets that wiggle with cheer,
In a world where imagination's free to appear.

With a sparkle, the dusk paints a canvas anew,
As dreams prance like rabbits, through the night's gentle dew.
So let's sip from the joy that the rafters can bring,
In the attic where laughter and memories sing.

The Silence of Forgotten Corners

A broom in the corner awaits its parade,
With whispers of dust bunnies, quite homemade.
The silence can giggle, as shadows convene,
In corners neglected, but bright and serene.

Old shoes tell stories of dances and woes,
While cobwebs divulge the secrets they chose.
A sock puppet argues with a forgotten glove,
In a duel of whispers, the quietest love.

The shelf has a grudge against all things that roll,
A marble uprising; it plays the old soul.
And sunlight peeks in like a curious cat,
To listen and laugh at the tales on the mat.

So here's to the quiet where laughter is found,
In the stillness of corners, where joy spins around.
Let the silence be golden, where stories unfold,
And the humor of life gets a grip on the old.

Secrets in the Sill

In corners where the dust bunnies play,
A mouse hosts parties at the end of the day.
Underneath the window, all secrets unfold,
Raccoons swipe snacks; they're lively and bold.

The curtain chats softly, a gossiping breeze,
With stories of antics from curious keys.
The sill is a stage for mischief and cheer,
Where the small things gather and laugh without fear.

Traces of Time in the Framework

The frames creak softly, recalling old times,
As squirrels practice acrobatics and climbs.
Nuts stashed in nooks where the sunlight won't reach,
They plot their next heist, plotting sneaky speech.

A spider spins webs, a complex ballet,
As dust motes dance lightly, come out to play.
The walls have old stories, both silly and grand,
Each mark tells a tale from this lively land.

Enclosures of Silence

The attic is quiet, though whispers abound,
Where ghosts of old toys have decided to sound.
A teddy bear giggles, a doll strikes a pose,
They reenact dramas nobody knows.

In boxes of memories piled high to the brim,
Old letters are tangled, their edges are grim.
Yet laughter rises up from the musty old air,
As ev'ry old token dances without care.

The Space Between Memories

In the gap on the stairs where the light tends to skip,
A gnome does gymnastics, a whimsical trip.
Forgotten old shoes, now seats for the ants,
While socks have a gathering, donning their pants!

The shadows are busy, they juggle the past,
While echoes of laughter along hallways cast.
In this charming chaos, so silly, so spry,
Life's trapped in a waltz, just passing us by.

Beneath the Surface of Sound

In the quiet, a creak sneaks a giggle,
A mouse joins the band, can you hear it wiggle?
The floor sings a tune, a mysterious song,
While the light bulb hums, "Oh, get along!"

Dust bunnies dance, wearing hats made of fluff,
Whispering secrets, all cheeky and tough.
The walls chuckle low, with a wobble and shake,
As old echoes play, for nostalgia's sake!

And up in the rafters, a squirrel's encore,
Plays marbles with thoughts that bounce off the floor.
With joy we're surrounded, parts hidden from view,
Where laughter resides, and the silly shines through!

So let's turn up the fun, let sounds be our guide,
In the silence, a ruckus of whimsy can hide.
For every soft whisper, there's greatness that looms,
In the tiniest spaces, life joyfully blooms!

The Soundtrack of Silent Spaces

In the corners, a chuckle, perhaps a brief cough,
The kettle's soft whistle, as if to scoff.
Bursts of laughter, in silence they swirl,
As tick-tock of clocks play out the wild whirl.

The dog's distant snore orchestrates the mood,
While shadows do tango, a marvelous brood.
Faint giggles erupt from beyond the closed door,
Even silence, it seems, is a tune to explore!

The fridge hums a lullaby, sweet and absurd,
While the curtains sway gently, not saying a word.
In the stillness, a riddle of noise yet unheard,
With echoes of nonsense, the laughter is stirred!

So crank up the quiet, let the silence resound,
For in every still moment, there's mischief abound.
In the air, a symphony, mostly unseen,
The soundscape of spaces, where joy's evergreen!

Junes Dusting the Eaves

Junes tiptoe lightly, dust motes in tow,
Shaking off cobwebs, putting on a show.
The sun beams a smile, with winks and with spins,
As the roof drips laughter, where sunshine begins.

A squirrel runs circuits, round poles and the beams,
What's real and what's jest spills into our dreams.
As wind chimes tickle, laughter dressed in cheer,
While shadows roll over, and goodness draws near.

Giggles of raindrops play tag with the trees,
As June's gentle charms write their adorable tease.
With bees doing ballet, nature's soft hum,
Awareness awakens, and we join in the fun!

So catch the odd whispers that bloom in the air,
For joyous July waits, with events rare and fair.
Where secrets and silliness blend in the eaves,
In Junes dusting laughter, oh how blissfully weaves!

Lament for the Unseen

Oh, the voices unheard, just lurking around,
In the folds of the floorboards, snug underneath ground.
They crackle with mirth, they giggle and sigh,
Completely oblivious as moments drift by.

I hear them complain of lost socks and such,
They mourn for the crumbs, oh how they miss lunch!
In the closet, they prance, with a gentle fade,
Oh, what a performance, how grandly they're played!

A ghost of a joke floats, it stumbles, it slips,
While the ceiling joins in, with chuckles from trips.
Their revelry bounces on laughter so clear,
Yet only the brave can glimpse their sly cheer!

So raise a toast high, to the joyful unseen,
To the hats made of shadows, never quite keen.
For laughter, it seems, knows no bounds, nor scene,
In the realm of the quirky, where silliness beams!

Secrets in the Eaves

A squirrel's stash of acorns hides,
Along with old love letters, it bides.
Mice hold parties, making a fuss,
While ghosts play cards on a bed of dust.

Cobwebs hang like grandma's lace,
Spiders waltz, a creepy grace.
There's laughter echoing from above,
As the rafters whisper tales they love.

Old shoes dangle, doing the tango,
With mismatched socks, like a strange fandango.
They kick and stretch, oh what a sight,
Drifting slowly into the night.

In the corner, a hat begins to rise,
Full of secrets and ancient sighs.
The eaves, a stage for quirky dreams,
Where silliness flows in glowing streams.

Echoes of the Celestial Space

A bird sings jazz from a high perch,
While the stars gossip, no need to search.
The moon chuckles, playing the fool,
As owls debate the rules of cool.

Cosmic dust dances with a beat,
Comets join in with a tap of their feet.
Galaxies giggle in endless parade,
While planets jump rope in the celestial shade.

Asteroids roll with a playful grin,
Trading jokes as they spin and spin.
Chuckling nebulae puff up in glee,
As they share tales across the wide sea.

In this vast stage of cosmic delight,
Laughter echoes soft through the night.
Stars twinkle back, a wink from afar,
In the joyous theater of the bizarre.

Dusty Dreams in the Cracks

In dusty crevices, dreams take flight,
Whispers of kittens, oh, what a sight!
A sock finds love with an old, lone shoe,
While dust bunnies frolic, a fluffy crew.

Cracks in the walls hold secrets tight,
While everyday stuff joins in for a fright.
Coffee spills tales from the morning rush,
As leftovers quibble in a silly hush.

Old toys reminisce, sharing a laugh,
While the spoons compete for a dance-off half.
A button dreams to be a flying ace,
Circled by crumbs at a raucous pace.

From these shadows, the shenanigans bloom,
Where laughter erupts, chasing away gloom.
In every crevice, a cheerfully dance,
Where dust and dreams find their chance.

Hidden Tales of the Joists

The joists whisper secrets, muffled and clear,
Of parties thrown by those who disappear.
With tiny dance floors in an unseen nook,
Where tiny toes play and giggles plook.

Wooden beams hold stories, both funny and odd,
Like the time a cat took a tumble—oh, what a fraud!
They chuckle at ghosts who've lost their way,
Trying to make the sun turn to gray.

A family of spiders set up camp inside,
Throwing wild raves on the wooden slide.
They twirl to a tune only they can hear,
Throwing confetti of dust, spreading cheer.

Here lies the essence of mischief and fun,
As the joists bear witness to all the run.
With laughter that echoes where shadows roam,
They weave together a whimsical home.

Dusty Secrets Beneath

Beneath the floor, where nobody peeks,
A colony thrives, with gossip that speaks.
Dust bunnies dance, in a waltz full of cheer,
While lost socks conspire, sharing tales of the year.

Mice hold court, on crumbs they have found,
Debates about cheese are the talk of the town.
A rogue spider spins yarns, while laying her web,
Of the sock that escaped, how brave he's become.

Forgotten old toys, with stories to tell,
An army of soldiers, will guard their old smell.
Each creak in the night, is a whisper, a jest,
Of secrets and laughs, that lay still but blessed.

So next time you step, on those boards made of pine,
Remember the fun, that folks leave behind.
A life full of anecdotes, laughter and sighs,
All hiding below, while the world walks on by.

The Quiet Life Above

Above in the rafters, where cobwebs do bloom,
Are secrets nonchalant, each given more room.
The birds host a concert, of chirps and of tweets,
While squirrels judge style in their furry retreats.

A calm that does settle, like dust on a shelf,
The light filters through, all alone by itself.
In the stillness of air, one can hear the odd sound,
A creak! A sigh! Life's jokes all around.

Occasionally, laughter floats in from below,
The rhythm of chaos in a soft ebb and flow.
A ceiling that gleams, with its shimmery paint,
Above all the ruckus, the wood beams just faint.

So raise up your head, look closely and see,
The humor in quiet, life's sweet reverie.
For up high where it's quiet, fun waits with a grin,
A place where the stories of laughter begin.

In the Cracks of Old Wood

In splits of the timber, no one deems to explore,
Lies a bank of old jokes, behind any door.
The termites are chuckling, they've built quite a hive,
With puns about woodwork, they keep things alive.

Old nails tell of battles, of projects begun,
Of hammocks swaying and laughter in sun.
Each knothole a portal, to laughter it's tied,
A gathering place where old spirits abide.

The planks shift and groan, like an old friend so wise,
Sharing a secret with a wink in their eyes.
Amidst all the creaking that lingers and drifts,
Lie treasures of giggles, and memories of gifts.

So next time you notice the wood that you tread,
Think of the stories, where humor has spread.
For in the old cracks, a party does thrive,
Trust me, dear friend, the wood beams are alive!

Silence Between the Joists

In spaces of stillness, where shadows take hold,
Lurk secrets and chuckles, both timid and bold.
The joists form a bridge, to laughter unsaid,
A vibrant exchange, while the world rolls ahead.

A chair in the corner has seen better days,
With cushions that laugh at their fraying arrays.
And up in the silence, where echoes remain,
Mysterious figures play charades without shame.

They chatter in whispers, of life and of fluff,
While dust motes giggle, their dance is enough.
Each creak of the wood, a meaningful jest,
An inside joke, that is hidden but blessed.

So venture indoors, where the quiet does reign,
And tune in to whispers, of wittiness gained.
For in the stillness, where laughter concedes,
A world of simple joy is sown, it proceeds.

Flights of Dust in the Sun

In the dappled light they dance,
Little specks in a wild prance.
Chasing shadows, taking flight,
Laughing softly through the twilight.

Mice slide by with pops and squeaks,
As dust bunnies play hide and seek.
Each footfall sends them swirling high,
Like tiny ghosts that float and fly.

Once a broom made a fine escape,
Chasing dust on its smooth tape.
Yet the dust, it wouldn't stay,
Said, "Not today, I'll play your way!"

So let them swirl and spin around,
In the golden sun they're bound.
With laughter echoing from each nook,
A silly dance in every book.

The Language of Empty Rooms

Whispers float on silent air,
Walls recall tales of gaps and wear.
Each echo holds a cheeky grin,
As if laughter stirs within.

Chairs wobble with secrets bold,
In corners where adventures unfold.
A table once dressed up in lace,
Now craves a wild, playful embrace.

Curtains flutter as they chat,
About a cat or maybe a bat.
Each creak of wood, a knowing quip,
Shared between every hidden slip.

In this realm where silence plays,
Words bubble up in funny ways.
Rooms giggle with a soft delight,
Their stories spun both day and night.

Whispers of the Attic

In the attic, dust settles deep,
Old toys and dreams take their sleep.
A globe once spun 'round the world,
Now just awaits a laugh unfurled.

Mice tell tales of lost old shoes,
Rats debate if they'll sing the blues.
A trunk holds secrets painted bright,
Each label a chance for delight.

Forgotten hats with feathers bold,
Whisper laughter from days of old.
What stories do cobwebs weave?
If only, we'd stay and believe.

As shadows play on walls so bare,
Each quiet corner holds a dare.
A nosebump joke or a ghostly tease,
In this space, we're sure to be pleased.

Shadows Beneath the Stairs

Beneath the stairs where whispers hail,
Crickets chirp out a funny tale.
Spiders knit their webs with care,
As shadows wiggle, unaware.

An old shoe jokes, "I'm not alone!"
Declaring that it has its own throne.
Dust mites giggle with every step,
Each landing a comedy prep.

In this nook, the giggles grow,
From ghostly friends we barely know.
With each patter of passing feet,
They revel in a rhythmic beat.

So tiptoe close and lend an ear,
For in the shadows, life's full of cheer.
You might just catch a silly song,
Beneath the stairs, it won't feel wrong.

Stories Resting on Old Beams

Up in the rafters, the dust bunnies play,
Telling old tales in a funny way.
A squirrel once slipped, with a nut in his paws,
And landed with laughter, deserving of applause.

The creaks share secrets of mischief and glee,
Of cats doing ballet up high on a tee.
While echoes of laughter dance in the air,
These high-flying fables, without any care.

Old boots up above are now hats for the mice,
They've thrown a grand party, and it's not very nice.
With crumbs from the kitchen strewn all on the floor,
They tap-dance to stories of legends and lore.

The beams carry whispers of laughter and cheer,
Of clattering dishes and friends drawing near.
So if you should listen, you might hear the sound,
Of memories stored in the wood all around.

The Heartbeat of the House

The wall clock ticks with a humorous beat,
As dust motes waltz on invisible feet.
A spider spins tales of romance and dread,
Chasing flies dreaming of a life instead.

In the kitchen, spoons fight a battle for fame,
While pots cling to stories that all sound the same.
The fridge hums a tune, a mischievous one,
With leftovers plotting a madcap run.

The floorboards squeak like they're part of the jest,
As the cat joins the dance, a curious quest.
Each creak and each shuffle, a slapstick routine,
In this house of whispers where laughter is keen.

Beneath the eaves where the shadows may loom,
The heartbeat of fun keeps the place full of room.
For in every corner, there's joy to be found,
In this whimsical house, where the silly abound.

The Embrace of Dimness

In corners where shadows chuckle and sigh,
The dimness is where the old spirits lie.
A broom on a journey, with plans to escape,
Rides on the back of a legendary tape.

The nightlight's flicker, a disco ball's glow,
As wishes are whispered, both timid and slow.
A haunted old chair throws a comical fit,
As it creaks and it groans, doing improv a bit.

The cobwebs cling on, with style and grace,
Draped like fine lace on a lady's face.
A book on the shelf tries to give you a wink,
Filled with stories of merriment, far more than you think.

In this playful gloom, where laughter takes flight,
A funny old ghost shares a joke with the night.
So tiptoe through laughter as shadows conspire,
For dimness is bright when humor's the fire.

Reverberations of the Past

The old piano sits, with keys made of dust,
It plays a funny tune, just because it must.
Each note a reminder of joys that once were,
Of socks on the floor and the cat's crazy purr.

Pictures on walls, with smiles so wide,
Watch as the antics from childhood collide.
A dog with a hat, a pig doing ballet,
Each frame a snapshot of silly display.

In the attic, a trunk holds secrets untold,
Of dresses that twirl and stories of old.
A pair of old shoes, with memories rife,
Danced around corners, bringing laughter to life.

As the echoes of giggles weave through the air,
The past clings to moments, both funny and rare.
For in every heartbeat, there's joy that will last,
In the reverberations of stories amassed.

Secrets Wrapped in Ages

In a creaky house of whispers and tales,
Lies a cat who steals socks without fails.
Old chairs gossip where they lean on the wall,
And the dust bunnies leap—oh, they're having a ball!

A box in the attic with letters from couch,
I found one from Grandma, it was worth a crouch.
She hid her old secrets in flour and spice,
Said a recipe's lost if you're not very nice!

Under the bed, where old toys can play,
Is a worn-out book that's missing a page.
It tells of the time a giant's shoe roamed,
And how little elves found a place to call home.

So here's to the things that we stash away tight,
In the laughter of memories, they come in at night.
With a wink and a wiggle, they dance through the air,
In a world full of giggles, who needs to beware?

Where Memories Maybe Linger

Upon the shelf, there's a jar full of smiles,
With candy from summers gone by for a while.
There's a photo of me climbing the tree,
But the branch said, 'No' and I tumbled with glee!

The tick-tock of clocks seem to chuckle and tease,
As I trip on memories like toys on a breeze.
There's a band-aid lost on the top of the stairs,
Hidden safely amongst all my childhood affairs.

A jar of marbles, old, cracked, and bright,
Played the role of planets one warm summer night.
Now they roll under beds, with no plan nor scheme,
While the dust motes dance in a forgotten dream.

The pantry's a treasure, with secrets untold,
A half-eaten cookie, all moldy and bold.
Caught in the snackings of nights long ago,
Reminding me sweetly, 'You reap what you sow!'

Lantern Light on Hidden Corners

With a flick and a flash, the lanterns will glow,
Illuminating echoes of when time was slow.
There's a broom that plays hopscotch upon the floor,
And dust motes declare they still want to explore!

In the corners so dark, where the shadows reside,
A sock puppet party, with laughter as guide.
They giggle and banter, they don't dare to sleep,
In the crevices tucked, where secrets they keep.

A mouse on a mission, sneaks cheese without sound,
While the pantry performs in a very grand round.
It's a cupboard cabaret, a zesty delight,
With a pickle in top hat, putting on quite the sight!

The lanterns are flickering tales of the past,
Of laughter and antics, like shadows they cast.
Here's cheers to the whimsy, to all things that play,
In the glow of the night, as the lanterns sway!

The Soft Breath of Breathable Walls

The walls hum a tune, or maybe it's me,
A serenade played by the old family tree.
With echoes of laughter and faint whispers of love,
These beams sing their tales from the heavens above.

A wallpaper blushes with stories in print,
Of cats in bold hats with a highly skilled glint.
They strut through the hallways and prance down the stairs,
While the light bulbs chuckle over all of life's cares.

There's a tickle somewhere behind cracked plaster beams,

Where memories flow like sweet buttered dreams.
The closets hold secrets with giggles and sighs,
As the buttons and ribbons share whispered goodbyes.

So here's to the spaces that cradle our years,
That hold all our giggles, our sorrows, and cheers.
In every soft breath that the walls seem to share,
Is a heart full of memories, light as air!

The Weight of Days Above

Laughter drips from ceiling cracks,
Echoes of mischief linger back.
Dust bunnies dance on wobbly beams,
As we chase our wildest dreams.

Sunlight spills like a spilled drink,
Tickling the spots where shadows blink.
Each creak a joke, each crack a pun,
Floating like bubbles in the sun.

We balance atop our towering thoughts,
Swapping stories that time forgot.
Old paint chips whisper in delight,
While floors rumble with playful fright.

Gravity giggles, heavy with fun,
Each day above weighs a ton.
Yet, somehow we rise, giggling still,
Under the weight of a whimsical thrill.

Lurking Pasts in Quiet Spaces

In corners, shadows chuckle and grin,
Where memories shyly scurry in.
A squeaky chair hums an old tune,
As if hiding a mischievous boon.

Cobwebbed tales find their way out,
Winking at us, full of doubt.
The ghosts of clumsiness linger here,
Stumbling on laughter and old fear.

Behind the walls, the mischief brews,
Time's jokesters in shoes that confuse.
Lurking lightly, they float and spin,
A dance of giggles we can't help but join in.

Memories peek from behind aging wood,
With glances so sly, they know they could.
In quiet spaces, hilarity grows,
With every creak, the past still glows.

Whispers of Old Wood

The planks conspire with a sly grin,
Sharing secrets of what has been.
They chuckle at tales of stumbles past,
Holding laughter that just won't last.

Wooden voices crackle with cheer,
Tales of clowns who dared reappear.
In their rings, the echoes play,
As children's giggles swish and sway.

A playful knock sends echoes round,
Where silliness grows from the ground.
Each knot holds laughter, every ridge a jest,
In the heart of the building, we find our rest.

So let the stories tumble and weave,
For old wood speaks to those who believe.
With every whisper, a memory spins,
Telling us laughter always wins.

Memories Stored in Aisles

In dusty aisles, where we can hide,
Jokes are stacked, side by side.
Each book a treasure, a tale untold,
With whispers of laughter, bold and old.

Rattling shelves echo a laugh,
As shelves play games in the past's craft.
Mismatched volumes form a funny crew,
They peek and giggle at me and you.

In corners, stories choose to sprawl,
With quirky characters causing a brawl.
Lost in pages, we tumble and sway,
Collecting the whimsy that won't fade away.

Memories stored where humor abounds,
In playful notes and colorful sounds.
Each aisle, a dance, a silly affair,
Where laughter is stored, free as air.

Ghosts in the Glimmering Gaps

In corners where shadows love to dwell,
The poltergeists dance with a jingle bell.
They knock on the walls, play tag with the light,
While the cat just stares in a mix of delight.

A tap on the ceiling, a thud on the floor,
What's that? Oh right, just the ghosts wanting more.
They sip on the echoes and laugh at the fuss,
Who knew the afterlife could be such a plus?

With each little creak, they begin to conspire,
To start up a game near the old attic fire.
They whisper and giggle, it tickles my ears,
Oh, what fun it is to have ghostly peers!

Next time I'll join in, or so I decree,
To prance with the spirits and drink ghostly tea.
Who knows what may happen, what tricks we might find,

When laughter and shadows get tangled entwined?

Hushed Conversations in Wood

The floorboards are chattering, wood on wood chat,
About who lost the race, was it Sammy or Pat?
They lean in for secrets, in whispers they share,
While squeaky old beams drop the news with a flair.

One says, 'I heard a ghost slid on by,
With rickety shoes and a very loud sigh!'
The shutters all shudder, the windows join in,
Oh, those crafty old floorboards, they're up for a spin!

A joke about dust bunnies, oh what a delight,
Fluffy little mischief-makers creeping at night.
The tales they exchange make the rafters all shake,
While I sit by the fire, amazed at their break.

When thunder rolls in, they hush and they pause,
With giggles suppressed and a silent applause.
The stories continue when the storm passes by,
As wood joins with wood in the midnight sky.

Sounds Crashing Like Fragments

Clatter and bang, there's a ruckus upstairs,
I wonder if Morty is breaking his chairs.
A crash and a roll, what's he found this time?
Oh look, it's a toy, just a part of the rhyme!

The ceiling fan spins, its blades humming low,
Swinging the dust into glittery show.
A thud from the attic, it's a game, can't you see?
The old boxes are fighting, as spirited as me!

A crash makes me wonder, what else is afoot?
I check on the fridge, but it's just the old soot.
Every sound's a story, every bang brings a laugh,
It's the house playing tricks, a mischievous gaff!

So next time you hear that loud comical boing,
Just know it's the house trying to join in your song.
With sounds crashing wildly like fragments of cheer,
Each echo's a friend, always welcome and near.

The World Above and Below

Upstairs in the lounge, there's a party tonight,
With laughter that tumbles and dances in light.
The floor shakes with joy, the walls join the spree,
While the basement just grumbles, 'Where's all the glee?'

In the kitchen, a spatula stirs up some fun,
While pots and pans clatter till day is undone.
The fridge tells a story of leftover plight,
While the ceiling lamp flickers, igniting delight.

The cellar feels grumpy, with shadows that pout,
'What's happening up there? Come share, don't miss out!'

But who could resist a wild, jovial sound,
With laughter that echoes, it's bliss all around.

So here's to the layers, the stories they weave,
A party above and a basement that grieves.
In this house full of humor and quirky retreat,
We dance with the laughter, our lives incomplete.

Unwritten Echoes of the Hearth

In corners where the dust bunnies hide,
A squeaky chair that creaks with pride.
The cat's a judge, with a knowing glare,
  On a throne of fluff, beyond compare.

Dishes stacked high like a game of Jenga,
A dance of chaos, oh what a benga!
Mismatched socks seek a partner to pair,
In the land of lost things, do we even care?

Leftovers whisper from halfway 'round,
In the chilly fridge, a joke profound.
The spoon's a singer; the fork's a clown,
In this kitchen show, no one's wearing a frown.

As laughter rings through, an echo in time,
Beneath this roof, life's silly rhyme.
Every bump and giggle, a thrilling spree,
In this heart of chaos, we're wild and free.

The Pulse of Enclosed Spaces

In tight corners where the shadows play,
A sock puppet party brightens the day.
The fridge hums a tune that's hard to hear,
While the broom tap dances with much cheer.

Old diaries boast of a crush so bold,
With doodles of dreams in stories told.
Every pile of clutter, a treasure chest,
Full of giggles hiding from the rest.

A cupboard door squeals with a neighbor's joke,
While cobwebs linger like a shy folk.
If walls could chuckle, what tales they'd weave,
Of mischief makers who still believe.

So let's toast to chaos that rules the game,
In enclosed spaces, nothing is the same.
With laughter echoing off every wall,
Life's whimsical charm encircles us all.

Threads of Life Interwoven

In a patchwork quilt of snippets and threads,
Life's odd little stories are winding their spreads.
A pair of mismatched shoes share a secret laugh,
While the dust motes dance like they're on a path.

Tea bags plot scheming as the kettle roars,
Socks unite for a rebellion against chores.
Slightly chipped mugs hold tales of delight,
Crafting warm memories, soft and light.

Mismatched utensils hold each other's hand,
In this culinary circus, oh so grand!
Every crumpled napkin, a diary page,
Speaks of silly moments that will never age.

So gather 'round the table, lift your glass,
To the threads of life that weave and amass.
In this quirky fabric, our joys often swell,
With laughter and love, we weave quite well.

The Language of Stillness

In the silence where the creaks reside,
A tick-tock clock reveals its hidden pride.
Dust bunnies chatter in a soft retreat,
While the room's full of whispers, oh so sweet.

A shadow slips by with a giggle and grin,
As the old chair winks, "Let the fun begin."
Every rustle of leaves tells a jolly tale,
In the hush of the moment, no one will fail.

Stale popcorn thoughts do a jig on the floor,
In the quiet, they bounce and always want more.
A sleepy cat dreams of adventures grand,
Chasing fanciful moments around the land.

So be still and listen to laughter unspool,
In the language of stillness, we're never a fool.
Hold on to the quiet where giggles collide,
In this serenade of life, let joy be our guide.

Nestled in the Gaps

In corners shared with dust bunnies,
Socks slide down, oh, how they run!
They twirl and dance, like little clowns,
Never a care, just having fun!

A spider spins a web so fine,
While popcorn kernels play align.
Who knew these nooks could be so bright?
Where laughter echoes through the night?

Between the shelves, the shadows play,
A world alive in the light of day.
Chasing dreams, they're out of reach,
These funny tales, floors shall teach!

Oh what a mess, the books, the shoes,
They coalesce, creating crews.
An army of lost things galore,
Whispering secrets on the floor!

Forgotten Dreams Underfoot

Underneath the wooden boards,
Forgotten dreams fly like a flock of birds.
They flutter out with a silly cheer,
Waving goodbye, no need for fear!

In the shadows, a lost toy giggles,
Bouncing around, trying to wiggle.
Missing its owner, it rolls around,
In the laughter, it's surely found!

Old magazines, huddled and shy,
Whispering jokes as they pass by.
They flip their pages, a comic scene,
Telling the tales that once had been.

With every creak, secrets unfold,
As stories of mischief delight the bold.
A whole world of laughter, just a foot away,
Where happiness and chaos love to stay!

Echoing Heartbeats Above

In the rafters, a party rages,
Silly echoes like turned pages.
Tiny footsteps, a tap and a thump,
Could it be ghosts, or just a jump?

Mice dress up in tiny suits,
Tapping their paws in clever hoots.
They waltz and twirl with utmost glee,
Creating a show just for me!

The wind chimes sway with a giggle,
As the house begins to wiggle.
A chandelier sways with style and grace,
Inviting all to this wild space!

Laughter hangs thick like tree roots,
Bringing together all quirky fruits.
With each heartbeat of the attic's song,
Who knew the laughter could be this strong?

The Stillness of Forgotten Rooms

In silent rooms where laughter lingered,
A cat peeks through, gently fingered.
Countless memories float like balloons,
As dust settles and in silence swoons.

The old chair groans under the weight,
As stories unfold like an open gate.
Lost in time, with wrinkles to share,
These friendly whispers fill the air!

Lurking around, the shadows dance,
Inviting dust to join the prance.
A game of hide-and-seek begins,
With laughter echoing, the room grins!

A forgotten shoe is making plans,
To organize a bash with her new pals.
While misfit cushions snicker and tease,
In this stillness, it's joy that frees!

Echoing Lives of Years Past

In hidden nooks where shadows creep,
Old memories dance and secrets leap.
Each creak and groan tells tales untold,
Of boots and broomsticks, of laughter bold.

A sock once lost, now found with glee,
Rats waltz wildly like it's a spree.
The cat gives chase with a flick of its tail,
While old granddad snores, his stories frail.

Dust bunnies bounce like they're in a race,
Challenging each other, a furry embrace.
Time's clumsy footsteps echo in delight,
As the past flips through pages, worn yet bright.

Once a graveyard of dust and dread,
Now a circus where dreams are fed.
With every squeak, a new laugh rings,
In this house of echoes, a joy takes wings.

Flickers of Light through Gaps

Sunbeams peek through cracks in the wall,
Playing tag with dust, having a ball.
Laughter hangs sweet in the morning air,
As shadows shimmy without a care.

The old lamp flickers, a cheeky muse,
Whispering secrets, sharing news.
A lightbulb's joke lost in its glow,
Makes the room chuckle, just so you know.

Rats hold meetings in dim little spots,
Debating cheese heists and fanciful plots.
A flick of the tail, a bastion of cheer,
In the midst of the chaos, we hold them dear.

Fan blades spin tales of times gone by,
While cobwebs serve as the grandest spy.
From light to dark, surprises abound,
In gaps of the house, laughter is found.

The Hidden Heart of the House

The fridge hums softly like a heartbeat,
As leftover lasagna embraces defeat.
Beyond its door, a feast so grand,
With pasts and futures in every hand.

Behind the curtains, flirts of the breeze,
Waltzing with dust, managing to tease.
The clock chimes loudly, it's time for a snack,
Tick-tock jokes abound in this unpredictable track.

Under the stairs, a treasure chest waits,
Full of mismatched socks and old birthday plates.
Laughter erupts from the closet, oh dear!
A ghost in a tutu is dancing near.

With every creak, a chuckle is born,
In this heart of the house, a joy is worn.
Each corner chosen, where fun never parts,
We celebrate life, in our peculiar arts.

Silhouettes of Dreams in the Air

Late at night, shadows perform a play,
On the walls and floors, they dance and sway.
The moon grins wide, a lopsided grin,
As dreams slip through the cracks, where fun begins.

The old broomstick leans with a wink,
Ready for flights—just don't overthink!
A pillow fight waits in a giggly reprieve,
Fuzzy silhouettes that weaves and weaves.

When the floorboards creak, it's the sound of mirth,
As wishes take flight, celebrating their birth.
A dream catcher hangs, catching laughter so bright,
In this playful abode where magic ignites.

With every breath of wind, tales unfold,
Of playful sprites with hearts of gold.
In shadows that stretch, our laughter still flies,
Beneath the stars and the watchful skies.

www.ingramcontent.com/pod-product-compliance
Lightning Source LLC
Chambersburg PA
CBHW062108280426
43661CB00086B/327